AIDS

HOW IT WORKS
IN THE BODY

LORNA GREENBERG

A FIRST BOOK

FRANKLIN WATTS

NEW YORK   LONDON   TORONTO   SYDNEY

Cover photographs copyright © : Photo Researchers Inc.:
both right (Chris Bjornberg), top left (National Cancer Institute/Science Source),
bottom left (Omikron/Science Source)
Photographs copyright © : The Stock Shop Inc./Medichrome/Howard
Sochurek: pp. 6, 13 top right, 25, 28; Photo Researchers, Inc./SPL: pp. 11 left,
13 top left, 13 bottom right (all CNRI), 11 top right (Dr. Tony Brain/David
Parker), 13 bottom left (Biozentrum), 15 (A.A. Dowsett), 21 (University of
Medicine and Dentistry of New Jersey), 36 top (Blair Seitz), 41 (Chris
Bjornberg), 42 (NIBSC), 45 top (CDC), 45 bottom (Prof. Luc Montagnier), 51
top (Will & Deni McIntyre); AP/Wide World Photos: pp. 17, 36 bottom,
51 bottom; NIAID/NIH: p. 32.

Library of Congress Cataloging-in-Publication Data

Greenberg, Lorna.
   AIDS : how it works in the body / Lorna Greenberg.
     p. cm.—(A First book)
  Includes index.
  Summary: Examines how the AIDS virus invades the body
and affects its immune system.
   ISBN 0-531-20074-4
   1. AIDS (Disease)—Juvenile literature. 2. HIV infections—
Juvenile literature.—I. Title. II. Series.
  RC607.A26G7 1992
  616.97′92—dc20   91-28620 CIP AC

CONTENTS

AIDS
HOW IT WORKS IN THE BODY

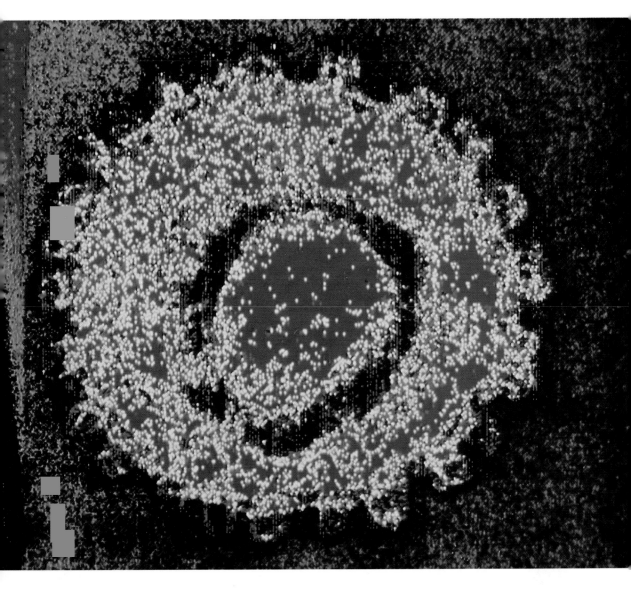

An enlarged, colorized view of HIV—the
human immunodeficiency virus

A NEW DISEASE

In the late 1970s a new disease seemed to appear from nowhere. The disease—later named HIV disease—was frightening and mysterious and seemed impossible to fight.

Thirty years earlier a major problem had been polio, a disease that could strike suddenly and cause crippling, or death. And 200 years ago another disease, smallpox, left many people very sick or dead.

Smallpox and polio no longer cause much illness or death. Scientists have been able to discover what causes them and have built strong walls of protection against them. As for this newer disease that causes AIDS, we are still in the middle of the battle against it. And no one knows how long this battle will last.

The name "AIDS" was developed to describe what doctors could see was happening in the disease. *AIDS* stands for *acquired immune deficiency syndrome*. "Acquired" means picked up or gotten sometime during a person's life rather than inherited. "Immune deficiency" means that the person's *immune system* (the body's defenses against disease) does not work as well as it should. "Syndrome" is a group of symptoms, or signs of illness, that usually appear together. The AIDS group of symptoms showed that something was damaging the immune system, and thus undermining the body's own defenses against disease.

HIV disease and AIDS have been seen in over 100 countries. The World Health Organization estimates that between 8 and 10 million people have become infected with HIV. By the year 2000, as many as 40 million people will probably have been infected.

To start the battle against AIDS, one of the first steps was to discover what caused it. Fortunately, as we'll see in the next chapter, scientists have successfully taken that important step.

THE CAUSES OF DISEASE

Every part of our world is full of life. Besides all the plant and animal life we see around us, we are also surrounded by countless tiny living things. They fill the air, rest on every surface, multiply on an uncovered glass of milk, feast on a scraped knee. These are the *microorganisms,* or small life-forms, that share our world. They are usually too small to be seen without magnifying lenses or microscopes.

Some microorganisms can be helpful, and we need them to get inside the body. They help digest food, produce vitamins, and may perform other functions. Others can live quietly, in a corner of the intestine for example, and cause no harm. But some microorganisms, if they invade the body and start multiplying, can make us sick.

We can call all the different kinds of disease-causing microorganisms *pathogens* (from Latin words meaning "to cause suffering"). Pathogens are organisms that move into other life forms and cause disease. Bacteria and viruses are the most common and most important kinds of pathogens. Some others are yeasts and protozoans.

BACTERIA

Bacteria are one-celled organisms. Each bacterium is a tiny living cell wrapped up in a tough cell wall. Through a microscope, we can see that some bacteria are shaped like straight rods. Others are ball-shaped and others are spiral-shaped. Each bacterium can perform basic life functions: it can take in nutrients, make proteins, and then grow and divide in half to reproduce itself.

If a bacterium moves into a body (the body is known as the host) and settles there, it can multiply in the millions in just seven hours. All this may happen while the host peacefully sleeps. Some bacteria may perform useful tasks. Others may produce *toxins,* or poisons, which can cause disease or

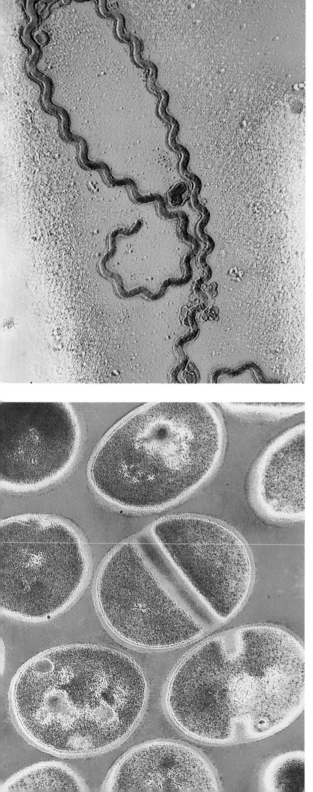
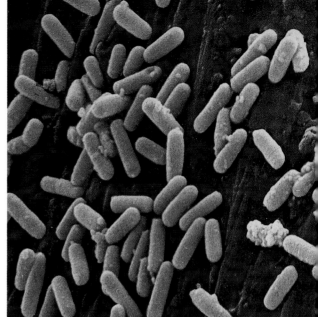

The bacteria shown here in the shape of spirals, rods, and spheres are all examples of one-celled organisms that can multiply in the body.

damage or destroy body cells. That is when signs of illness appear, perhaps strep throat or a pimple or even tuberculosis. If the person gets very sick, doctors may be called in to help the body fight the infection. Because bacteria stay outside the cell membrane of the host's cells, medicines can work against them while leaving the healthy cell alone.

VIRUSES

Viruses are much smaller and simpler than bacteria. They come in many different shapes: spheres, rods, six-sided crystals, one-handled rolling pins, bullet shapes, and more. They are tiny—too small to be seen except with electron microscopes, which can magnify from 40,000 to 100,000 times. Scientists measure viruses by "nanometers" (a nanometer is a billionth of a meter). Viruses range from 17 to 300 nanometers, so even the largest are too small to imagine. One drop of blood might hold 3 million red blood cells; each blood cell could hold a thousand viruses.

The viruses shown are all too small to be seen with the naked eye but are powerful enough to cause disease. Clockwise from the top left are the measles, polio and yellow fever viruses, and an adenovirus, a cause of nose and throat infections.

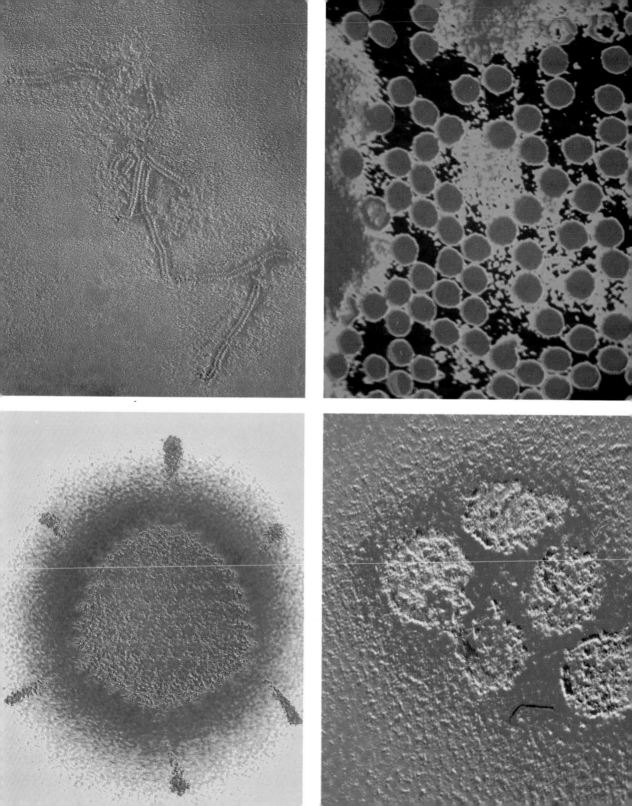

It is hard to think of these tiny viruses as living things because they don't really seem alive. On their own, they can't perform any life functions. They can't use nutrients, make energy, grow, or reproduce. They are just tiny bits of matter. But viruses can cause over fifty kinds of human diseases—colds, flu, chicken pox, measles, and, as scientists were to discover, AIDS. Let's take a closer look at a virus, what it is, and what it does.

LOOKING AT A VIRUS

In some old horror movies, a brain is kept alive in a jar on a laboratory shelf, waiting for the brilliant scientist to find it a human body. Once put inside the body's head, the brain could take over and force the body to do what the brain wanted. A virus is a little like that brain that needs a body. It needs a host, a living cell it can move into and force to do all the things it can't do for itself.

Small and very simple, viruses are little bundles of a substance called nucleic acid. This nucleic acid is wrapped in a protein coat. The nucleic acid of a virus carries the genetic information, the instructions, for making new viruses. But without a body—with no cytoplasm or cell material, no cell wall, no nucleus—the virus cannot produce protein and grow and reproduce. The virus has to find a living cell to live in and command.

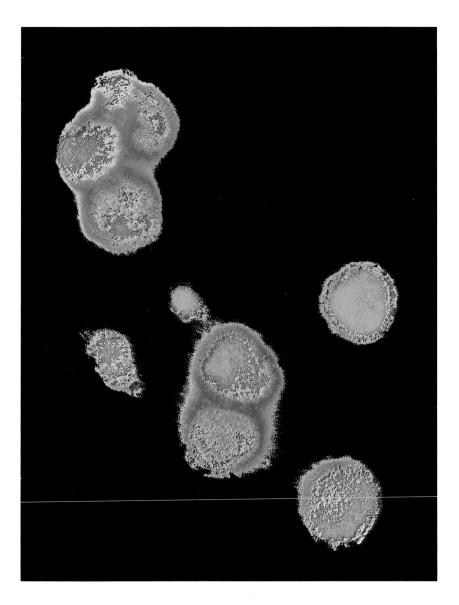

Viruses, such as the flu virus seen in this photo taken through an electron microscope, need to find host cells to perform their life functions.

Viruses seem to be fussy. They don't move into just any cell, but seek out specific targets. Most can invade only one specific kind of living organism. Chicken pox, flu, and measles viruses invade only human bodies; cowpox virus invades cows, and distemper virus invades dogs. Once inside the organism, the virus needs to find just its right kind of cell. It moves through the bloodstream until it bumps into the specific kind of cell it can enter. Flu virus can move into cells in the breathing passages, while mumps virus can invade glands in the cheeks and under the chin.

Once a virus finds the kind of cell it needs and moves into it, it takes control. The virus's nucleic acid chemically tricks the cell into following its orders. The cell is now a slave. Instead of reproducing itself, it is forced to produce copies of the invading virus, along with new protein coats for those viruses. The cell has been made into a virus factory.

Soon—in anywhere from an hour or two to a day

In 1985 HIV, the virus that leads to AIDS, was identified by researchers in the United States (top) and by researchers in France (bottom).

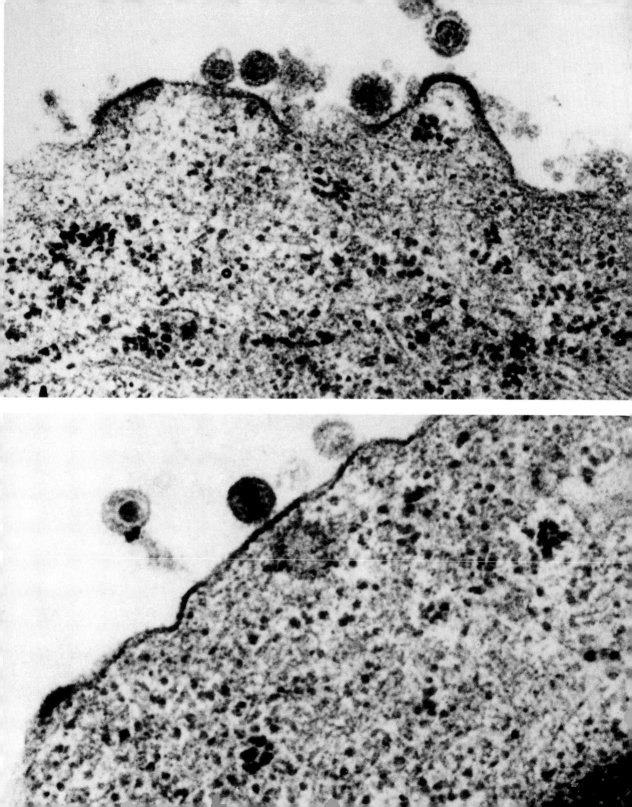

or two—the host cell is filled. At that point it bursts open, releasing many new viruses into the organism's bloodstream. The host cell usually dies, and then each new virus finds another host cell to invade. Now the virus-carried infection—perhaps measles or flu—has invaded the body cells and is ready to attack. And since viruses can move inside the cells (unlike bacteria), medicines don't usually help against them. They can't attack the virus without attacking the cell, too.

When researchers began to study HIV disease, the way the disease appeared and spread from one person to another seemed to be important clues. This meant that the cause was some microorganism—probably a virus. Working from what they already knew about other virus infections, and from blood and cell samples from people with HIV disease, researchers identified a virus that attacked cells in the body's immune system. We now call this virus *HIV,* for *human immunodeficiency virus.* This is the virus that causes AIDS. Identifying it was an important step in the fight against AIDS.

DEFENDING THE BODY

With all the disease-causing viruses, bacteria, and other pathogens lined up against us, who, or what, is on our side? How do we stay healthy most of the time?

THE FIRST LINE OF DEFENSE

In any battle, the first defense is to keep the enemy outside. The body's first line of defense is the skin. The head, trunk, arms, and legs—all the outside surfaces of the body—are covered by a thick and sturdy layer of skin. The body's inside surfaces—in the mouth, nose, esophagus, intestine, vagina, urethra, and rectum—are protected by a lining of moist skin tissue called *mucous membranes*. This skin is thinner than the outside skin. The breathing passages have extra protection from small, hairlike structures that trap foreign material. Germ-killing chemicals in tears and in saliva, and acids in the stomach and intestine, also work to protect the body from invasion.

But sometimes microorganisms do get past these first defenses. Tiny breaks in the mucous membranes may allow a flu virus to be breathed in. Or a bacterium may enter through a scraped knee. Once inside the body, however, the invaders come face-to-face with an army of defenders—the billions of cells of the immune system.

AN ARMY OF DEFENDERS

The immune system is the body's national guard, ready to be called up to fight off any enemy. It is a network of different types of cells—each with separate jobs, that work together to protect the body. If bacteria or viruses get inside the body, they can use its own resources to multiply and flourish. The immune system works to destroy these invaders or keep them from growing and causing infection.

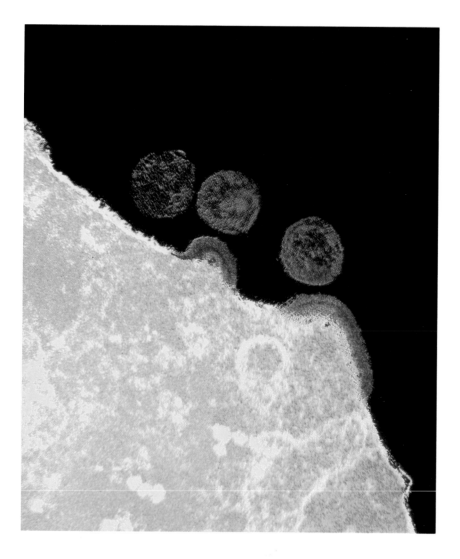

Once inside a cell in the body, a virus can
multiply. Here HIV has infected a cell and has
used the cell's resources to make the new
virus particles shown in red.

In the days of castles and moats, sentries at the gates asked, "Who goes there?" If the intruder did not know the password, the alarm was sounded and guards rushed to defend the castle. The immune system has sentries, too.

Certain cells of the immune system are able to recognize what belongs to the body and what is foreign to it. They can tell the difference between what is part of the body and what is an invader.

Sounding the alarm, alerting the immune system to an invader's presence, is the first part of the body's response to an invasion. Once an invader is detected, the second defense stage is begun. Other cells of the immune system produce chemicals that identify whatever invader has appeared. In the third stage of the immune system defense, some immune system cells mount an attack against the invading pathogen.

IMMUNE SYSTEM SOLDIERS

The soldiers of the immune system—the cells that do the work of protecting the body against disease and infection—are several dozen kinds of white blood cells. They work together to identify invading pathogens, prepare defenses, and then attack the enemy.

LYMPHOCYTE FORCES

Lymphocytes are small white blood cells. There are many kinds of lymphocytes that make up a very important group of the immune system army. The group includes the cells that can identify substances as foreign, and then start to build and direct defenses against them. Lymphocytes all develop from cells in the bone marrow inside bones. Two main kinds of lymphocytes develop—*B cells* (or *B lymphocytes*) and *T cells* (or *T lymphocytes*).

B cells—the antibody builders   The first kind of lymphocytes are called B (for bone) cells because they move straight from the bone marrow into the bloodstream. Here they circulate with the blood through all the tissues and organs of the body, looking for foreign substances.

In certain places in the body—in the neck, armpits, groin, and some other spots—B cells collect in small, spongelike masses called lymph glands. B cells roam through the body. When a B cell meets an invader—perhaps a virus or a foreign chemical—it inspects it. Each invader carries on its outer surface particles of a particular shape. These serve as markers or labels and identify it. These particles are called *antigens*. The antigens give information to the B cells. This helps the B cells fight the invader. The B cells produce substances that may match the invader's antigens. The substance is an *antibody*.

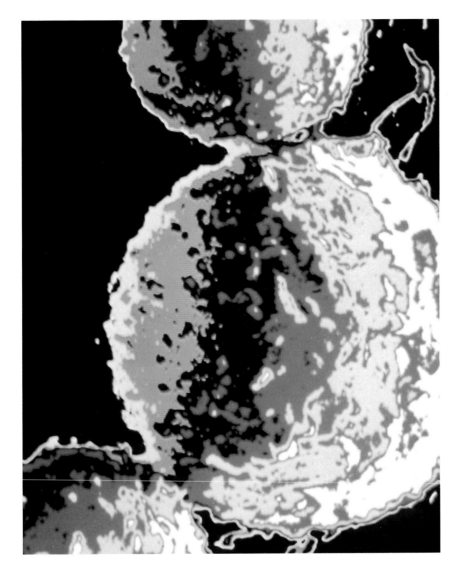

The small white blood cells known as
lymphocytes are the backbone of the
body's protective immune system.

Antibodies are the B cells' chemical weapons against invaders. When the antigen and the antibody meet, they can fit together, like a key inside a lock. Once that happens, chemical reactions occur that bind them together. The antibody is clamped onto the virus; the virus is paralyzed and can't invade new cells. The B cell that produced the needed antibody starts to multiply. In this way, many more antibodies can be made to fight the invader.

When this battle is over and the invader is destroyed, some of the antibody-producing B cells stay in the body as memory cells. If the same enemy, perhaps a chicken pox virus, ever invades again, the immune system is already armed against it with the memory of the chicken pox antigen. The person will not get chicken pox again because the immune system is ready to fight it off. We say the person is immune to (exempt from or protected against) that disease. B cells can start to fight back so quickly that the enemy can be wiped out before an infection begins.

T cells—the regulators The second part of the white cell army is made up of the T cells. These lymphocytes are called T cells because, after leaving the bone marrow, they spend some time in the thymus gland. The thymus gland is a spongy organ that lies below the throat. It produces chemicals that prepare the T cells for doing their jobs just as the B cells do theirs.

The T cells are divided into separate squads, each with a different task. The *helper T cell* squad sends chemical messages to the B cells, identifying the invader and ordering them to multiply and start producing the antibodies to fight that invader. The *suppressor T cell* squad sends the message to stop or slow down (suppress) antibody production when the invader is defeated. The *killer T cell* squad can destroy cells carrying invaders. When some killer T cells meet an invader, they can send out chemicals that kill it. Other killer T cells call in another group of immune system soldiers—the phagocytes.

PHAGOCYTES: THE EATING CELLS

Along with the lymphoctyes (B cells and T cells), another group of white blood cells joins the battle against invaders. These are large white blood cells called *phagocytes*. Their name comes from Latin words that mean "eating cells," and the phagocytes do "eat" invading pathogens. Phagocytes circulate all through the bloodstream and tissues of the body. If they meet an invader, they surround it.

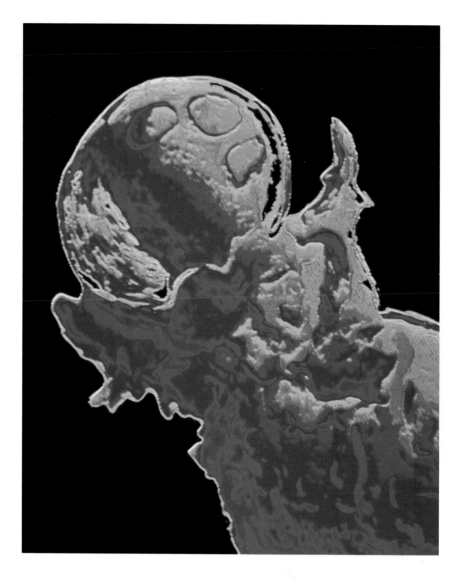

In this photo taken with an electron
microscope, a phagocyte surrounds
and destroys a cancer cell.

The chemicals of the phagocyte destroy it, just as the chemicals in the stomach and intestine destroy (digest) food. A *macrophage* is one type of phagocyte. Its name means "big eating cell."

These groups of white blood cells work together to fight off disease. Most of the time they are successful. The immune system can conquer most viral diseases. Medicines usually only help the sick person to feel better, or sometimes slow down the virus so it can't multiply as quickly. This gives the immune system cells time to produce enough antibodies to fight off the infection. The dangerous viruses of the past, such as the smallpox virus, were those that raced through the body so quickly that the body's immune system had no chance to fight back.

5

HIV AGAINST THE IMMUNE SYSTEM

The immune system can provide strong defenses against bacteria, fungi, viruses, and other pathogens that can cause infections. But of all the human body's enemies, HIV—the human immunodeficiency virus—is one of the most dangerous.

HOW HIV IS SPREAD
Some viruses are *transmitted,* or spread, easily. If a person with a cold sneezes out viruses, the person in the next seat may breathe them in. They may then

pass through the mucous membranes in the nose to get to the host cells they need in the lungs. There they flourish and multiply, spreading the infection. Like a cold, mumps and chicken pox viruses are also spread through the air. These diseases are very contagious, or easy to catch.

Other viruses are not spread this way. The rabies virus is spread when an infected dog or squirrel or other animal bites through a person's skin. HIV is not transmitted through the air either. This virus can be spread only when an infected cell or a virus from one person directly enters the blood or body cells of another person.

HIV can live only in certain body fluids: in blood and semen (fluid containing sperm) and, in smaller amounts, in a woman's vaginal secretions (fluids produced by glands inside the vagina). Tears, saliva, and other body fluids and feces may carry the virus. But in these the amount is so small that there is little chance of infection. When there is a transfer of body fluids—especially blood or semen—from one person to another, the virus may be carried along in the fluid. Once it is transmitted to another person, it then has to get inside the blood system through a cut or tear.

Once HIV enters a person's body, the person is "infected." That means the body is carrying the vi-

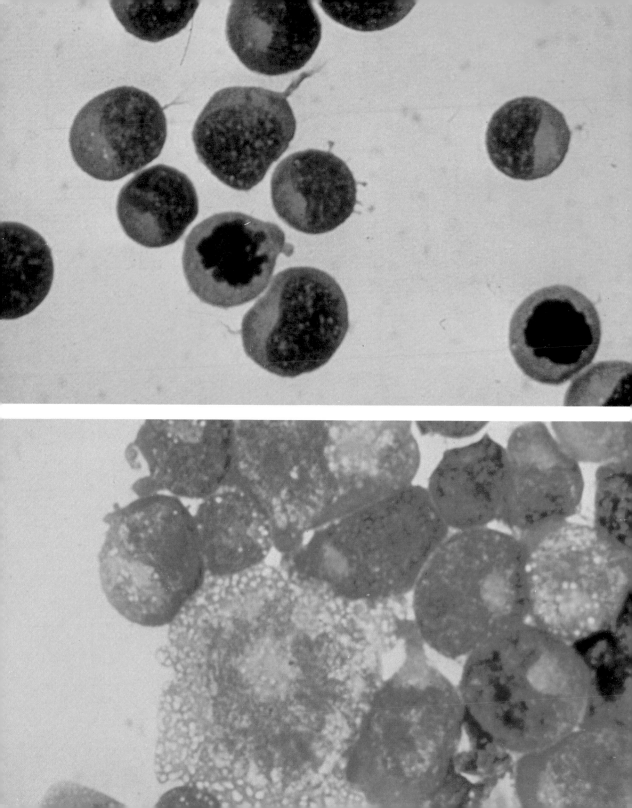

rus, probably for life, and can transmit it to others. It doesn't necessarily mean the person will develop the disease called AIDS.

HOW HIV ENTERS THE BODY

Body fluids are transferred from one person to another in three main ways, so these are the ways in which HIV can be spread. They are through sexual intercourse, by blood-to-blood contact, and from an infected woman to her unborn child during pregnancy or in childbirth. HIV is not spread by touching or even kissing someone who is carrying the virus, by swimming in the same pool, or by breathing the same air.

Through sexual intercourse In sexual intercourse, the virus may pass from one person to another if body fluids (semen and vaginal secretions) are exchanged. The virus may then pass through tiny breaks in the mucous membranes—the soft skin tissue that lines the openings to the body—or may be absorbed directly into the bloodstream.

The normal human T cells on top are healthy and help to protect the body. The T cells on the bottom have been infected by HIV.

In the United States, AIDS first appeared among groups of homosexual men (men who choose other men as sexual partners), and some people thought it was a disease of homosexuals. We now know that anyone can get AIDS. In other parts of the world AIDS is as common among women as among men. It is generally people's behavior that puts them at risk for AIDS.

By blood-to-blood contact Before we knew much about HIV infection, or AIDS and how it is spread, some people were infected when they had transfusions of HIV-carrying blood after an accident or an operation. People with hemophilia (a disease in which the blood does not clot) were sometimes infected when they were given blood products that carried HIV. Many of the school-age children who have AIDS were infected by the blood products used in treating their hemophilia. Since 1985 all blood and blood products used to treat sick or injured people are tested to be sure they do not carry the virus. Infected blood is destroyed. It has always been safe to donate blood because the needles used are sterile, used one time only, and then thrown away.

Blood can be transferred from one body to another in other ways. HIV can then be carried along. Intravenous drug users, people who inject illegal ("street") drugs directly into their veins, sometimes share their needles with other addicts. The first user's blood might remain on the needle and be injected into the next user. If any virus is present in the first user's blood, it may enter directly into the next user's bloodstream.

When doctors and other health workers give patients shots or perform blood tests, they use new, sterile needles that are never used again, so there is no chance of spreading infection. But needles used for tattooing or ear or nose piercing might not be sterile. Razors or toothbrushes might carry traces of blood, so these should not be shared. Anything that might carry blood might also carry a virus. And open wounds or cuts in the skin could allow the virus to enter the body.

From an infected woman to her unborn child If an HIV-infected woman becomes pregnant, the virus may be transmitted to the developing fetus. The baby's and mother's nutrients and body fluids are shared during pregnancy and childbirth. The baby may then be born with HIV. Doctors believe that about 30 percent of babies born to HIV-infected women will be born with the virus. An infected mother's breast milk might also carry HIV.

HIV—the virus that causes AIDS—is not easily transmitted. Direct blood-to-blood contact (as

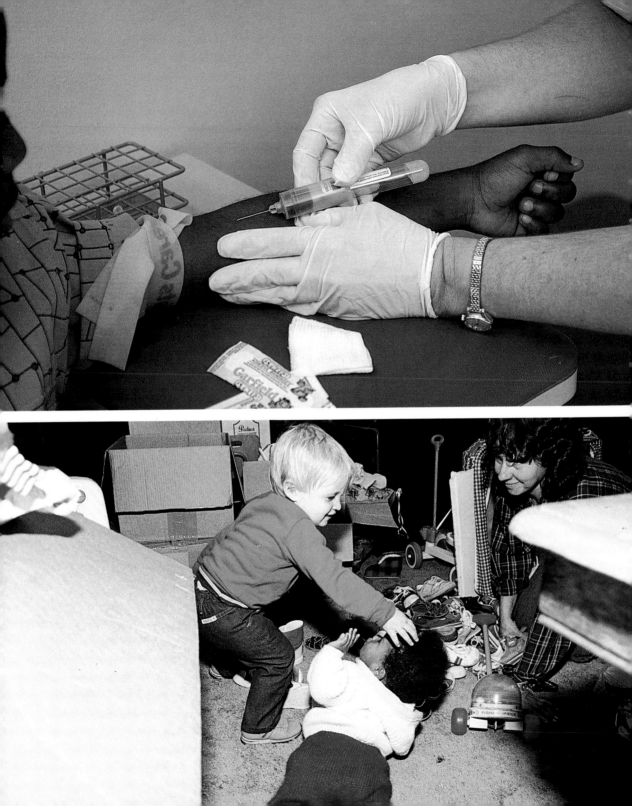

through needle sharing), sexual intercourse, and infection during pregnancy are the only known ways in which the virus can be spread. These ways of spreading the disease depend on people's behavior. We need to know what behavior is risky and puts us in danger of becoming infected. We can then control the risks.

Risky behavior includes injecting illegal drugs with shared needles, and exposing ourselves to direct contact with other people's blood or body fluids. Sexual intercourse can bring risks. Abstaining—not having sexual intercourse—avoids risks. Having sex with one partner who is not infected and is not an intravenous drug user reduces risks. Using condoms (thin latex-rubber sheaths worn over the penis) and spermicides (sperm-killing chemicals used in-

(Top) Careful precautions, which include sterile needles and protective gloves, are necessary safeguards against infection in health-care facilities. (Bottom) HIV is not spread through casual contact. At a child-care center a healthy youngster and a younger, HIV-infected child can play together without risk to the uninfected child.

ternally) may prevent the transfer of HIV. But these sometimes fail. "Safe sex" books and pamphlets provide more information about how to make sex less risky. "Safe sex" means sex with just one partner who has no infection.

HIV is fragile. On its own, outside the body, it can't live very long. Most virus particles will be damaged in a few hours. Soap and water, detergents, laundry bleach (a solution of one part bleach to nine parts of water), disinfectants, and heat treatments kill the virus.

For all people, understanding how HIV is spread is important. We need to be careful about behavior that can expose us to HIV, and we also need to know that we are not in danger when we walk down the street, visit a friend, go to school, play on the basketball team, swim in the community pool, share a lunch, or use a public toilet.

HIV IN THE BODY

HIV, the tiny but powerful virus, silently finds its way into the body. The person doesn't feel the attack. Weeks or months may pass with no signs of infection, although the person is now carrying the virus and can transmit it to other people. Often, at this stage, the person develops a case of what feels like the flu, with swollen lymph glands (lymph nodes), fever, night sweats, headaches, and a tired feeling. These symptoms usually disappear in a week or so, and the person may stay healthy for a long period—for as many as seven years, or even longer.

But the virus has not disappeared or been destroyed. It is inside the body, searching out the particular kind of host cell it needs. HIV seeks out the helper T cells of the immune system as its special target. It also looks for macrophages, some brain cells, and a few others.

HIV finds the host it needs by touch. The virus bumps into cell surfaces until it comes upon one with a structure on its surface that fits snugly into a "receptor," or groove, on the virus's own surface. The virus latches onto the structure and injects its nucleic acid into the host cell. The host is now under the control of the virus.

At some point, the cell is given a chemical signal to "turn on." (The signal might be triggered by an infection.) The virus orders the cell to start producing new viruses. These new viruses follow the genetic instructions that were carried in the virus's nucleic acid. Hundreds of small ball-like viruses grow out of the virus-factory host cell and the host cell then dies. The new viruses move into the bloodstream in search of their own helper T cells to invade. As each new generation of viruses appears, more and more host helper T cells and other cells are invaded and killed.

The helper T cells direct many of the activities of the immune system and help defend the body

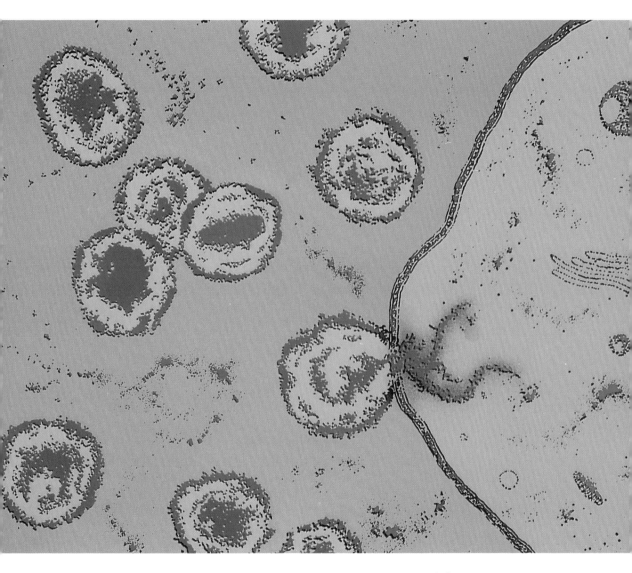

In this colorized photo, an HIV particle
has found a host cell and injects its
nucleic acid into the cell.

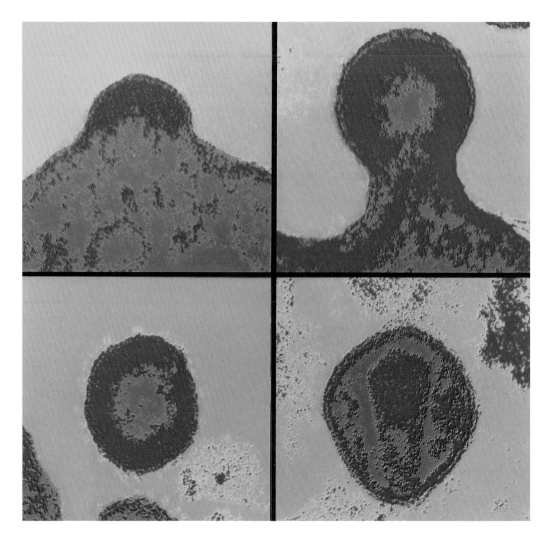

This series of colorized photos taken through
an electron microscope shows the formation of
an HIV particle. The virus first appears as a
small red bump on the surface of the
cell (top left). It then buds out (top right),
detaches, and moves away from the cell.

against infections. As they are killed, the immune system grows weaker. Other viruses invade nerve cells, liver cells, or lung cells and cause a lot of damage. But HIV may be the most dangerous virus of all because it destroys the very cells whose job it is to protect the body—the immune system cells.

Along with helper T cells, HIV also infects and damages macrophages. The B cells discover the invading virus in the bloodstream and start to produce antibodies against it. But with a shrinking population of helper T cells to direct them, the B cells cannot do their job well. Bit by bit, the immune system begins to crumble.

A large percentage of the people who are infected with HIV develop AIDS. After a while, the weakened immune system breaks down. Too many helper T cells have died; there are too many viruses in the body. The immune system defenders can no longer protect the body. Now pathogens that can't hurt healthy people move in to take advantage of the defenders' weakness. The infections they cause are called *opportunistic diseases*. The weakness of the immune system gives them an opportunity to enter the body and to grow.

One of the most common opportunistic diseases is *Pneumocystis carinii* pneumonia (PCP). This dangerous lung disease is usually seen only among people with damaged immune systems. It is caused by a small protozoan and the symptoms are a long-lasting cough, shortness of breath, chest pain, and a high fever.

Kaposi's sarcoma (KS) is a rare form of skin cancer. Large purple or brownish spots appear on the skin. While KS is usually a mild, slow-growing cancer, in AIDS patients it can spread much more quickly and is a serious disease.

Fungus-caused infections of the mouth and throat, tuberculosis and other lung diseases, hepatitis and herpes viruses, and bacterial diarrhea also strike when an immune system is damaged. And since the immune system is an important defense against the growth of tumors, AIDS patients often develop cancers.

Sometimes HIV uses brain or central-nervous-system cells to serve as hosts, as well as immune

(Top) HIV (the yellow spheres) invades and destroys T cells, leaving the body with weakened defenses against disease. (Bottom) A colorized photo taken with an electron microscope shows HIV particles that have entered a T cell. As the T cells are destroyed by the virus, the body becomes vulnerable to diseases.

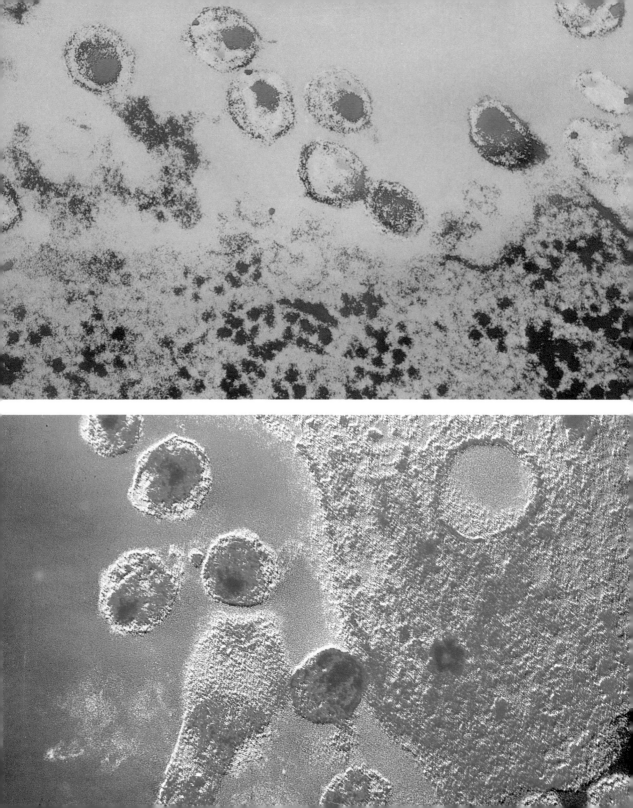

system cells. Memory loss, confusion, problems in speaking, standing, walking, and in other areas of motor control are symptoms of damage caused by HIV.

As HIV continues to spread through the body, the helper T cell population falls even lower. The infected person may develop more frequent and more serious infections. Doctors can treat some of the infections and diseases that affect a weak immune system. Antibiotics, other drugs, and medical treatments can help a person recover from an AIDS-related pneumonia or a fungus infection. The immune system, however, does not recover. Each new attack of pneumonia or other opportunistic disease leaves the person weaker. At this time there is no cure, and there is a high death rate for people with HIV/AIDS.

DIAGNOSING AIDS

Fever, swollen glands, and fatigue—the early signs of HIV infection—are also symptoms of flu, chicken pox, and other different and much less serious infections. AIDS can't be identified by any specific rash or symptom, so doctors look for pieces of information to show that a person is HIV-infected. Glands in the neck and armpits that swell and stay swollen for months for no reason are often a first clue. Another clue is an unexplained loss of weight. Fungus infections, Kaposi's sarcoma, PCP, and other opportunistic diseases are important signs, too. Since healthy people have two helper T cells for every suppressor T cell in their blood, a test that shows fewer helper T cells means something is damaging the immune system.

A laboratory test provides the most important information. If a person is infected with HIV, the B cells of the immune system begin to produce antibodies against the virus. The test examines a blood sample for antibodies to HIV. If they are present, the person is carrying the virus. A newer test, the Cetus test, is used to detect HIV itself in macrophages.

It is important for people to know if they are carrying HIV. The virus can be carried for years without any signs of illness. But through all that time, the carrier could infect other people. Another important reason for HIV tests is that drug treatments now being developed may slow or stop the spread of HIV within the body. It is helpful to start these treatments early, before much damage has been done.

THE OUTLOOK

When the first cases of the disease we now call AIDS appeared in the 1970s, it seemed as if a terrifying menace was shadowing our lives. What was this horrible new disease? What caused it? How could such a terrible disease appear so suddenly? Was it a plague? Would everyone get it? How could we protect ourselves against it?

Scientists in the United States and other countries began to try to solve the mysteries of the disease. Through the work of many researchers, some answers have been found. We know the disease is caused by a virus and that virus has been identified. We now know the symptoms of the disease and the pattern it follows. We know how the virus is passed from person to person and how it gets inside the body. We know how the virus reaches the immune system and cripples it, leaving the body open to opportunistic infections.

We now know a good deal about the disease and how it works in the body. This is what this book is about. But some parts of the AIDS puzzle are still missing. We don't fully understand all the workings of the immune system. And we don't yet have a cure for AIDS.

How to protect people from being infected by HIV, how to treat the diseases that attack AIDS patients, and how to cure AIDS are active areas of research today.

VACCINES AGAINST HIV

Some scientists are trying to find a way to wipe out AIDS by making people immune to, or protected from, infection by the virus that causes it. We have vaccines that give us immunity to other once deadly diseases—polio, smallpox, yellow fever, and more. Vaccines protect by using the immune system's own natural abilities. On page 24 we saw that when B cells find an invader, they produce antibodies to fight it off. After the invader is destroyed, some B cells that can produce the needed antibodies stay in the system as memory cells. They are ready to defend against infection if the same invader ever re-appears. Armed with these ready-for-action B cells, the body has immunity against that infection.

Vaccines provide people with immunity without exposing them to the dangers of the disease. Scientists working on HIV vaccines are looking for ways to get the immune system to create HIV antibodies. Successful vaccines could arm the body with antibodies to prevent infection by HIV. And they could strengthen immune defenses if the virus has already entered the body.

It would be too dangerous to inject people with a weakened or mild form of HIV. Vaccines for some other diseases, such as flu and measles, are made this way. Some researchers are experimenting with

(Top) When working on vaccines to fight HIV, researchers safeguard themselves by wearing protective clothing.
(Bottom) This photo shows a greatly enlarged crystal of AZT, the active ingredient in the drug Retrovir. Retrovir is used in the treatment of AIDS.

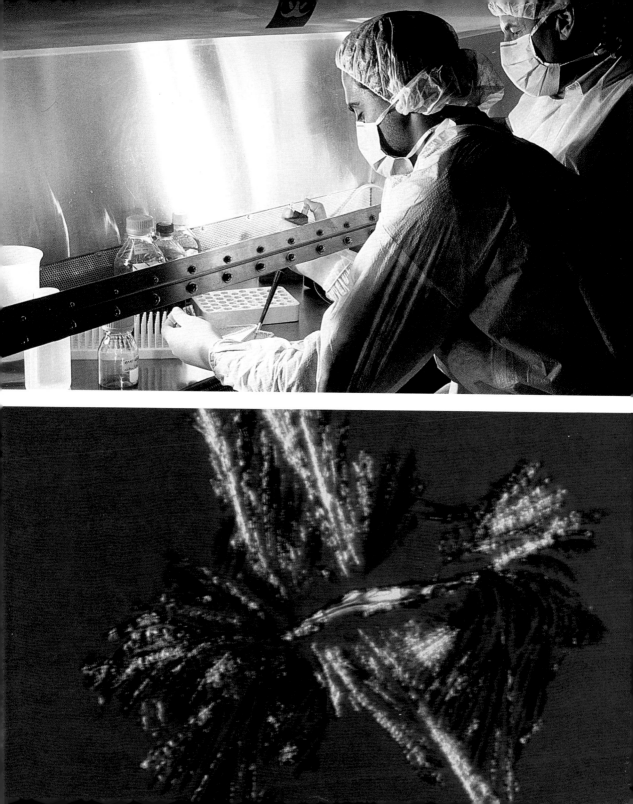

using parts of the virus; others are working with killed viruses. If a vaccine seems to work in a laboratory, it will need to be carefully tested to be sure it is effective and safe.

DRUGS TO HELP FIGHT THE VIRUS

Scientists in a number of research centers are working to develop "antiviral" drugs. These would kill HIV that has found its way into the body. Antiviral drugs interfere with the virus life cycle. Some prevent the virus from attaching itself to or entering a host cell. Others stop the host cell from making new viruses or from assembling and releasing viruses.

AZT, or Retrovir (zidovudine, formerly azidothymidine), is the major antiviral drug now being used by people with AIDS. It blocks HIV from ordering the host cell to produce new viruses. It does not cure HIV disease, since it doesn't kill the virus, but it slows the virus's progress through the immune system. It helps patients to feel better and live longer. Ribavirin is another drug that interferes with the production of viruses.

Nearly all drugs have side effects. For example, cold pills may make you sleepy or aspirin may upset your stomach. Antiviral drugs are powerful and may have powerful and dangerous side effects. AZT may damage bone marrow and some organs. Part of the task for scientists is to find drugs that are not as damaging.

The immune system produces natural chemicals. These include thymosin, which is made in the thymus gland, and interleukin-2, which is made by helper T cells. These help the immune system cells do their work. Some researchers are investigating whether these and other natural substances can help an infected immune system fight back against the virus, or perhaps even repair itself.

TREATING OPPORTUNISTIC DISEASES

While scientists work on vaccines to prevent HIV disease and on antiviral drugs to combat it, the search continues for better ways to treat the infections that move in to attack people with AIDS.

If a person with AIDS develops Kaposi's sarcoma or another cancer, cancer treatments such as chemotherapy, radiation, and surgery are used. Antibiotics, antifungal drugs, and combinations of drugs are used to treat other infections. These drugs are often effective, and the pneumonia or fungus or other infection is killed. But the patient still has AIDS. And in time another infection often appears.

THE OUTLOOK

Nearly every week newspapers report discoveries about the human immune system. Scientists are learning how the B cells are able to produce anti-bodies to fight any invaders. They are discovering how a virus can slip its genetic material into host cells. They are learning more, too, about how viruses and other invaders attack the immune system.

Today we are working toward an understanding of how a new viral disease like AIDS can appear. And, in many research centers, scientists are experimenting with ways to bolster the body's defenses and repair damaged immune systems. Their hope is that success in this search will bring a cure for AIDS.

GLOSSARY

AIDS (acquired immune deficiency syndrome). A disease that is caused by a virus that attacks cells of the immune system, leaving the infected person vulnerable to certain infections and cancers.

Antibody. A protein, produced by the B cells of the immune system, that circulates in the bloodstream and fights infection.

Antigen. A substance that stimulates the body's immune defenses to produce antibodies.

AZT (azidothymidine, now called zidovudine, trade

name Retrovir). An antiviral drug approved in 1987 by the U.S. Food and Drug Administration for treatment of AIDS.

Bacteria. One-celled organisms that sometimes cause infections.

B cell, or B lymphocyte. A type of small white blood cell that produces antibodies in response to the presence of an antigen.

Cancer. A disease in which body cells multiply out of control.

Condom. A protective sheath worn over the penis during sexual intercourse to prevent the passage of semen.

Helper T cells. Lymphocytes that stimulate B cells to produce antibodies.

Hemophilia. A rare hereditary disease caused by a deficiency in the ability to make one or more blood-clotting proteins.

Heterosexual. A person sexually attracted to people of the opposite sex.

HIV (human immunodeficiency virus). The virus that causes AIDS.

Homosexual. A person sexually attracted to people of the same sex.

Immune deficiency. A condition in which the body's immune defenses do not work properly.

Immune system. The body's natural system of defenses. Specialized cells and proteins in the blood and other body fluids work together to fight invading pathogens and cancer.

Immunity. The state of being protected against (immune to) a disease.

Infection. Invasion by a pathogen.

Interleukin-2. A protein, produced by helper T cells, that may help combat the AIDS virus.

Intravenous. Injected into or delivered through a needle into a vein.

Kaposi's sarcoma (KS). A cancer or tumor of blood vessels in the skin.

Killer T cells (natural killer, or NK cells). Lymphocytes that attack pathogens and cancer cells.

Lymph glands (lymph nodes). Small clusters of lymphocytes in the neck, underarm, groin, abdomen, and other parts of the body.

Lymphocytes. Small white blood cells that function in the immune system; includes B cells and T cells.

Macrophage. A type of large white blood cell that can engulf and destroy an invading virus or bacteria.

Microorganism. A life-form so small it can be seen only with a microscope.

Nucleic acids. Complex chemicals inside living cells and viruses. DNA and RNA are nucleic acids that carry the special genetic codes of the cells or viruses.

Opportunistic infection. A disease that is usually rare

but that is able to attack HIV-infected people because of their weakened immune systems.

Pathogen. Organisms that move into other life-forms and cause disease.

Phagocytes. White blood cells that can destroy invading microorganisms. A macrophage is one kind of phagocyte.

Pneumocystis carinii pneumonia (PCP). A rare type of pneumonia that sometimes strikes people with AIDS as an opportunistic infection.

Protein. An organic compound needed to build cells and tissues in all living organisms.

Semen. The mixture of sperm and sexual fluids produced by the male.

Suppressor T cells. Cells that suppress or slow down the B cells' production of antibodies.

Symptom. A physical change (such as fever) or a feeling that is the sign of a disease.

Syndrome. A pattern or characteristic group of symptoms.

T cell, or T lymphocyte. A cell that is processed by the thymus gland before it enters the bloodstream. Some groups of T cells have special immune system tasks. They signal other lymphocytes to attack invaders. They also help control how quickly the B cells produce antibodies.

Thymus. A small gland that lies below the throat. It processes lymphocytes into T cells.

Toxin. A poison that can cause disease or damage or destroy body cells.

Vaccine. A preparation (usually made from a modified virus or bacterial protein) that creates an immune response.

Virus. A tiny microorganism: a core of genetic material enclosed in a protein coat. Viruses can invade body cells and cause infections such as polio, measles, and smallpox.

Zidovudine. The newer name for the drug AZT.

FOR FURTHER INFORMATION

BOOKS

Armstrong, Ewan. *The Impact of AIDS*. New York: Gloucester Press, 1990.

Hyde, Margaret O. and Forsyth, Elizabeth H. *Know About AIDS*. New York: Walker & Co., 1987.

Knight, David C. *Viruses, Life's Smallest Enemies*. New York: William Morrow, 1981.

Nourse, Alan E., M.D. *Your Immune System*. New York: Franklin Watts, 1989.

Silverstein, Alvin and Silverstein, Virginia. *Learning About AIDS*. Hillside, N.J.: Enslow, 1989.

National AIDS Information Clearing House
Rockville, MD 20850
1–800–458–5231

National AIDS Network
1012 14th Street, NW, Suite 601
Washington, D.C. 20005
(202)293–2437

United States Public Health Services
AIDS HOTLINE 1–800–342–AIDS
              1–800–342–2437
              1–800–AIDS-TTY (for hearing
              impaired)

INDEX